To C...

Vikram M... a...

MW00888209

Lord of the Bubbles

AND
A MULTITUDE OF MANY
OTHER
FUNNY POEMS

SUITABLE FOR ALL AGES, TEMPERAMENTS, PROFESSIONS, CLIMATES, AND LATITUDES

*Hand-crafted Using the Finest
Organic Letters, Words,
and Oxford Commas*

*

*Featuring a Perplexed Cast of
Wacky, Weird, and Wonderful
Cartoon Characters*

*

*And Created for the Singular Benefit of
All Individuals with a Professed
or Unprofessed Interest in Poetry*

by

Vikram Madan

* Earnestly Illustrated by the Author *

Lord of the Bubbles: and Other Funny Poems by Vikram Madan
Copyright © 2018 Vikram Madan, All Rights reserved.

No part of this book may be used or reproduced in any
manner whatsoever without written permission from the
author except in the case of brief quotations embodied
in critical articles and reviews.

For information, contact the author via
www.VikramMadan.com

Madan, Vikram
  Lord of the Bubbles: and Other Funny Poems / Vikram Madan
Includes index.

ISBN-13: 978-1986885355
ISBN-10: 1986885356

1. Children's Poetry, American. 2. Humorous Poetry,
American. 3. American Poetry. 4. Humorous Poetry

Book Design by Vikram Madan.
No cartoon characters were harmed in the making of this book.

DEDICATED TO MY FAMILY
AND TO EVERYONE WHO
LOVES BOOKS

Acknowledgements

Many, many heartfelt thanks:
To my parents, for making me who I am; To my family Madhu, Jahnvi, and Jawahar, for their abiding patience, love, and support; To Vanessa Pepoy, for helping seed several poems in this collection; To Rebecca Davis, for observations that helped tighten up some of these poems; To Ed DeCaria, for organizing the annual March Madness Poetry Tournament where a couple of these poems first appeared; To Douglas Florian, for his continuing encouragement in the writing of poetry; To all the teachers, librarians, and school kids I meet on school visits, for continuing to love and enjoy poetry (and a special thanks to Ms. Heady's class of 2013-2014 for the poem 'A Riddle'); And to everyone who follows my work and fuels it with their enthusiasm and well-wishes!

Lord of the Bubbles

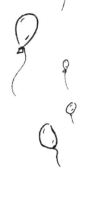

I ♥ BALLOONS

The thought of balloons always
Fills me with smiles
The sight of balloons has me
Grinning for miles

They lift up my spirits
They're cheery, they're bright
They make my heart flutter
And soar like a kite

I can't say I like
How they look, feel or smell
What has me excited is...

...How <u>well</u> they SELL!

HARD LESSONS

This Watermelon's rotten
  And icky to the core
I found this out the hard way
When I dropped it on the floor

This Apple's somewhat squishy
  And gooey to the touch
I found this out the hard way
When I handled it too much

This Nectarine is noxious
  And horrid to the taste
I found this out the hard way
When I bit it in my haste

This fruit basket's revolting
  I'd toss it 1, 2, 3
I found this out
      the hard way...

EEEW   POKE
        POKE

...All the fruit-flies disagree!!!

CAN'T SLEEP

I found it very hard to sleep
My Granny said, "Just count some sheep!"
I closed my eyes and counted sheep
But found I could not sleep a peep
I counted sheep, I counted goats
I counted horses eating oats
I counted cows and flying crows
I counted pigs arranged in rows
I even tried a goose and duck
But no, oh no, I've had no luck
I have not slept a wink or nod
Could it be that...

....my counting's flawed?

HELP! MISSING PET!

Please help, our pet has disappeared—
  We think she's gone astray
We fear she must be feeling weird—
  She's never been away!

We found the kitchen door ajar
  But no one saw her leave—
She could not have wandered too far,
  She's nearby, we believe!

She answers to the name of Rose
  And likes to hide in shrubs
She loves a pat upon the nose
  And craves a belly rub!

She might be cold (she's short on fur);
   She's timorous and shy
Be gentle if you do see her
   For noises make her cry!

She has a patch upon one eye
   She's mostly colored grey
She's such a little sweetie-pie...

... Please help find her today!

ATROCIOUS DIET

You never eat your carrots,
Your pasta or your beans
You feed the tot your cabbage,
Your spinach and your greens

You sneak into the kitchen
To steal the pies we bake
You stuff your mouth with cookies,
Your pockets full of cake

No matter what we're serving,
You're always seeking treats
You don't care if we scold you
Or confiscate your sweets

Your diet's so unbalanced
You'll turn into a mess
When will you learn to grow up?...

....That's anybody's guess!

A BURPPELLA

To prep for our performance
It's soda we must slurp
And though we love the sugar-high
What we want is the *BURP*

Our quartet is uncommon
Our talent is unique
We *BURP* our songs in harmony
With patented technique

We belch out all the pop hits
And oldies, hymns and such
Our friends adore our repertoire
Our teachers... not so much!

HOMEWORK MAYHEM

Jackie's homework lost her laundry
Jessie's homework chewed her ball
Jenny's homework chased her uncle
Six times to the shopping mall

Wilbur's homework nipped the mailman
Wesley's homework ate the car
Wendell's homework got a tattoo,
Grew long hair and played guitar

Mandy's homework gossiped gossip
Michael's homework trashed his place
Morton's homework robbed a bank and
Disappeared without a trace

If you think your homework's boring
That's a reason to be glad
Think of how much trouble you'd have
If your homework turned out bad!

BRONTOSAUR BALLET

When Brontosauruses perform
A Brontosaur Ballet
In little shoes and pink tutus
They dance all night and day
On giant knees, they flit like bees
They pirouette and play
And twist and twirl, and spin and swirl
And whirl and bend and sway
Their massive girth shakes up the earth
And takes your breath away
When Brontosauruses perform
A Brontosaur Ballet

When Brontosauruses perform
A Brontosaur Ballet
Perhaps it would be sensible
To stay out of their way!!!

FOUR TYPES OF PANDAS WE <u>NEVER</u> SEE

i.
The legs upon the **PANDA-PEDE**
Keep rolling with synchronous speed
A blur of motion – white and black
A slur of motion – front to back
Through grove and woods, through copse and trees
It ripples with relentless ease
Unless it trips… then down it goes
A cavalcade of tangled toes!

ii.
The **PANDA-ROO**, with leaps and bounds
Keeps bouncing-bouncing all around
Its rounded rump, with rumpus sound,
Goes thump-thump-thumping on the ground
There's nothing graceful to be found
About the way it bounds unbound
Thump-thump-thump-thumping on the ground
Thump-thump-thump-thumping all around
And in its pouch the kid **P-ROO**
Is probably thump-thumping too.

THUMP

THUMP THUMP

iii.

Those **PANDA-BOTS**, those **PANDA-BOTS**
They never amble, stroll or trot
Through snow and rain, through cold and hot,
They sit there rusting in one spot,
Looking like something time forgot.
Sometimes they lie down in a knot
Sometimes they snack on spoons and pots
But mostly they just sit and squat.
They don't do much, those **PANDA-BOTS**
If you can use them, take the lot!

iv.
Beware the
PANDA-SAURUS REX
Pretending to be cute
It nuzzles with
     its muzzle till
You feed it
     bamboo shoots
It lulls you into
     liking it—
     Then sits on you,
     the BRUTE!

*

ONE KIND OF PANDA WE <u>ALWAYS</u> SEE

PANDAS sit and chew and chew
Boring bits of green bamboo

GIZMO-YO

Boy, O boy,
  O boy-O, O
I have a fancy
  new Yo-Yo

It's shiny, sweet,
  and gizmo-fied
It's musical
  and amplified

There's blinking lights,
  a hi-res screen
With knobs and buttons
  in-between

With internet,
  and Wi-Fi too
There's nothing that
  it cannot do

Well, almost nothing,
  for you see
It just won't
  yo-yo easily :(

THE BUDDING ARTIST
A True Story

I drew a cat, a flying cat
They said, "How cute! A duck!"
I drew a duck, a quacking duck
They said, "Oh, look! A truck!"

I drew a truck, a monster truck
They said, "So sweet! A mouse!"
I drew a mouse, a mighty mouse
They said, "We love this house!"

I drew a bunch of squiggles
As angry as you please
I thought I'd leave them speechless but
They said...

FROG AND FROG
Poem Backwards A

log rotting a upon perched
frog lonely cheerless a lurched
"broke is voice my
croak only I
me with friends be to wants one no
be can sad as sad am I so"

bog the from voice-frog a rose then
"frog O, sing you heard first I when
jumped and skipped I
thumped-thumped feet my
log your on you join please I may?
frog O, you with croak me let, pray!"

replied frog the "joy O, gee O
"side my join please, ask to need no"
log that upon since ever and
frog and frog croak hand-in-hand

25

THE DESPONDENT DRAGON

My cave is dark and gloomy,
   my hoard is dank and cold
There's nothing much to do here,
   my best friend is a mold
The Crown Prince I abducted
   complains an endless bunch
Each dull and dismal dreary day
   I'm despondent by lunch

You want to save his highness?
   Please do so, I insist!
You want to steal my Treasure?
   I vow I won't resist!
My only stipulation–
   I pray you'll hear me through–
Is, take the gold and grumbler,
   and take **me** with you too!

BON APPETIT

I told them I was hungry
As HUNGRY AS A HORSE!
And that is why I sit here
Abounding with remorse

My plate is overflowing
But I'm at an impasse
They took me at my word and they
Served me OATS and GRASS!

TEACHER'S PET

The quintessential Teacher's Pet
  is always neat and proper
Her hair is combed, her face is scrubbed,
  her grades make her a topper

  She laughs at all the teachers jokes,
    she volunteers for tasks
  Her hand is raised the highest for each
    question teacher asks

    The other kids are envious of
      all her stars and 'A's
    They think the teacher favors her –
      "Why her?" they always say

      They don't know that she tries to be
        the best that she can be
      The quintessential Teacher's Pet,
        well I'm so glad she's ....

DOWN AT THE BARBER SHOP

The tortoise sighed "My hair is wild
And so out of control
It always looks unkempt, un-styled,
Which saddens my old soul"

"No matter how it's combed or brushed
It will not stay arranged
It's always thatch-y, patchy, crushed
I'm anxious for some change!"

"So Barber dear, let's have no doubts,
Please shave my noggin bare!"
—And that's all we can say about
The tortoise and the hair.

<u>Attention</u>

The next poem is for
Super-Villains only.
If you are not a *Super-Villain*,
please skip ahead to
Page 36.

DOOMSDAY MACHINES!!!

Doomsday Machines! Oh, yes! Doomsday Machines!
Serving your evil and dastardly schemes!
Smashing a planet into smithereens?
Come get a deal on our Doomsday Machines!

Freezing Rays! Melting Rays! Lasers and Beams!
Shrinking Rays! Growing Rays! Powered by Steam!
Spawning odd mutants by fiddling with genes?
Come get a deal on our Doomsday Machines!

Armies of Robots? Try Robo-Clone-2™!
Crossing the timelines? Use Time-Warp-4-U™!
Searching for saucers or stealth submarines?
Come get a deal on our Doomsday Machines!

Binding with Mind Waves?
                Get Hypno-gizer™!
Building a fortress?
                Try Qwik-Fort-Riser™!
Turning world leaders into figurines?
Come get a deal on our Doomsday Machines!

Anti-Grav-Cruisers or Space-faring Blimps?
Nanotech Bugbots or Super-Smart Chimps?
Evil computers? Buy six or eighteen!
Come get a deal on our Doomsday Machines!

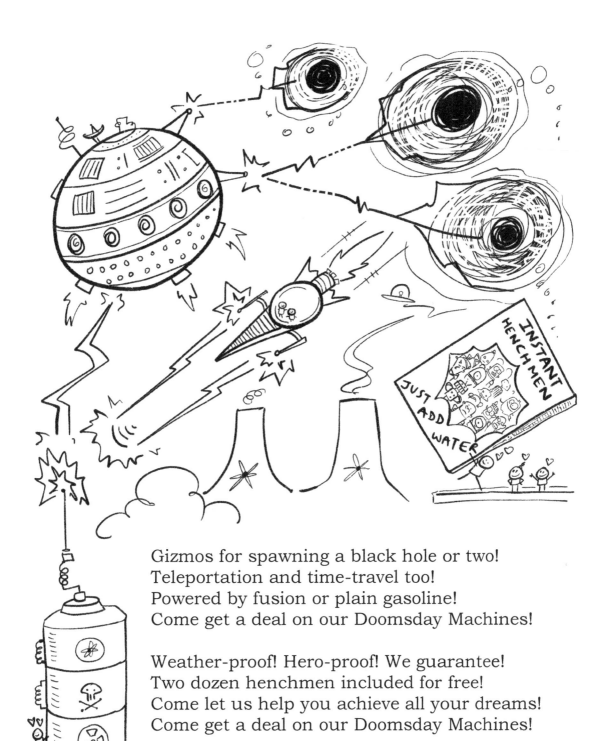

Gizmos for spawning a black hole or two!
Teleportation and time-travel too!
Powered by fusion or plain gasoline!
Come get a deal on our Doomsday Machines!

Weather-proof! Hero-proof! We guarantee!
Two dozen henchmen included for free!
Come let us help you achieve all your dreams!
Come get a deal on our Doomsday Machines!

Doomsday Machines! Oh, Yes! Doomsday Machines!
Come get a deal on our Doomsday Machines!

THE PEDDLER

Early each Sunday we jump from our beds
And wait for the peddler, the peddler of heads

We savor the smells as they waft up the streets
Heralding his cart overloaded with treats

He sets up his stall at the end of the square
And offers free samples to all who are there

There's soft ones and tough ones and crunchy and fried
There's smooth ones and rough ones with sweeties inside

He greets aunts and grannies out looking for sales
He gossips and guffaws, regales them with tales

His manner is charming, his prices are fair
His goods are delicious—his cart is soon bare!

On tables in kitchens all throughout the town
They gobble his goodies with nary a frown

And wave through the windows when he clatters by
And lick all their fingers and happily sigh…

Awaiting the next time they'll gorge on his spreads
The peddler, the peddler, the peddler of—

Wait, did I say *HEADS*????
Oops, I meant *BREADS*…! :P

FUNNY LOOKING

Grasshoppers are funny looking
Bendy legs and buggy eyes
As they sit there in the grasses
Scraping scratchy songs on thighs

We can marvel at their strangeness
When they're puny, tiny, small
But they aren't so funny looking…

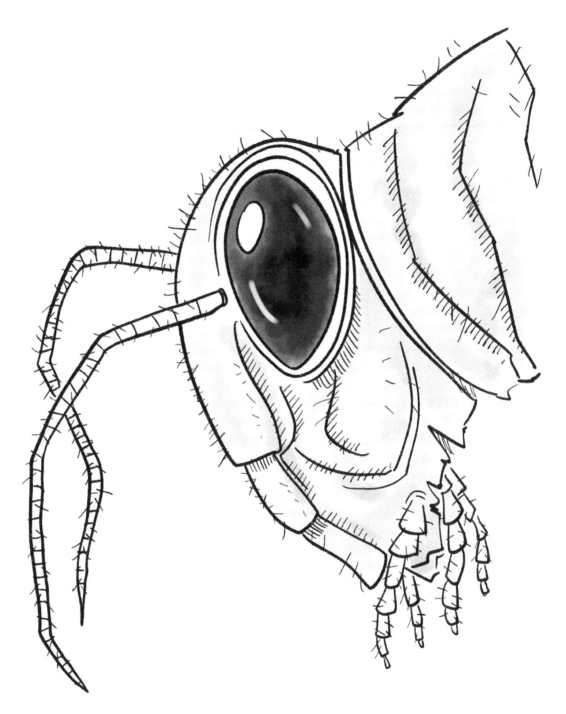

...when they're forty-two feet tall.

TOU-CAN-CAN

Can one toucan do the Can-Can?
   Can two do it too?
If two toucans do the Can-Can
   Surely one can too?

If just one of two can Can-Can
   What do two then do?
Do they Can-Can? Do they Can-Can't?
   I don't have a clue!

If two toucans cannot Can-Can
   Are they just tou-can'ts?
One can't, two can't, I can't, you can't
   We can't end this chant!

Author's Note: A Can-Can is a type of dance involving a lot of leg-kicking.

RAINING, RAINING

Raining, raining cats and dogs,
  We don't mind at all
Fish and fowl and toads and frogs?
  They can hail and squall!

Sheep and goat and pigs and boar
  All of those are fun...

41

...But when hippos start to pour
Then it's time to run!

WORLDS LUCKIEST GAL

I am cheery Miss Sal, the world's LUCKIEST gal,
   Even though things don't often go my way
In a bus, van or car I don't get very far
   Without ending up lost on some highway

Half the clothes that I wear simply tatter and tear
   While the other half fray and unravel
What I drop on the ground will then seldom be found
   (And I keep dropping stuff as I travel)

All my stockings have holes, all my shoes have no soles
  I misplace all my scarves and my mittens
When I go near a pet I break out in cold sweat
  For I know for a fact I'll be bitten

Be it rain, wind or sun, if I walk, skip or run,
  I will falter, and stagger, and stumble
If I'm going up stairs or I'm standing on chairs
  You can bet on your life I will tumble

I get stung by the bees when I nap under trees
  If I swim it's the fish who will nip me
And I try to stay clear of all scissors and shears
  For I haven't a doubt they will snip me

I catch colds when it's hot, any food I buy rots
  Why my pop has no fizz I can't explain
If I sit in a boat it will no longer float
  So I dare not embark on an airplane

If I dance or cavort, or I play contact sports
  I am sure to be battered or injured
Should you feed me a treat, be it salty or sweet
  All I taste in my mouth is fried ginger

I don't sleep well at night for I fidget in fright
  As my bedsheets and nightclothes are haunted
When I once won a prize, well to no one's surprise,
  It was something that nobody wanted

Now by now you must think I must be on the blink
  With a luck as afflicted as mine is
But I stay full of cheer every day of the year
Yes I feel tons of bliss, and my secret is this—
I have found a best bud whose luck is just as crud
So when trouble occurs, be it his, be it hers
We can conquer, divide, marching on side-by-side
Marching on mile-by-mile, trooping on smile-by-smile
  And that's simply as good as divine is...

Yes I'm cheery Miss Sal—the WORLD's LUCKIEST GAL!

RULE OF THUMB

A simple rule of thumb
That merits much repeating
Shampoo is for washing
And ketchup is for eating

THE RACE THAT WE LOVE

There's a race to be run with a spoon and an egg
   There's a race to be hopped in a sack
There's a three-legged race where they tie up your leg
   And then laugh when you trip on the track

There's a race to be run full of hurdles and snags
   There's a race to be run on your hands
There's a race where your head is inside a brown bag
   And they shout out commands from the stands

There's a race to be run where the slowest one wins
   There's a race where a baton is seized
But the race that we love and can't wait to begin…

49

...Is the race that combines all of these!

ALL OF US

Some of us are—*ACHOOO!*—sneezing
Rest of us sit here and cry...

...All of us, though, know we'll never
Make more Onion-Pepper Pies!

THE ROYAL SUP

The Royal tea in Royal cup
Awaits a dainty Royal sup
A Royal slurp, a Royal sip
Past Royal lip a Royal drip
Down Royal chin a Royal drop
On Royal dress a Royal plop
A Royal gasp! Then this decree:

NO ROYAL TEA FOR ROYALTY!

FACADE

The front of a Queen
Is calm and serene
And prim, and trim,
And sensibly neat
As fronts of all Queens should be...

The back of a Queen's
A chaotic scene
A mess, I guess
That takes a backseat
(Thank Goodness!—Don't you agree?)

PUMPKINS

Pumpkins are nifty for carving
And feeding to hippos and such
And making pies when we are starving
But juggling? Oh, gee, not so much!

SIR ALGERNON: THE SUPER SLEUTH

A Poem Inspired by T.S. Eliot

Sir Algernon's an upright hound:
    He's called the Super Sleuth—
For he's the trusty officer
    who shall uphold the Truth.
He's the epitome of police squads,
    the lawmaker's delight:
For where there is a scene of crime—
        Sir Algernon's on site!

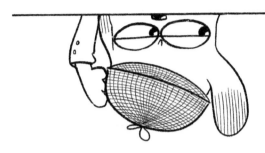

Sir Algernon, Sir Algernon,
     there's no one like Sir Algernon,
He catches those who break the law,
     he chases every crook and con.
His powers of deduction can
     fill lawbreakers with fright,
For where there is a scene of crime—
        Sir Algernon's on site!

You may lay low in a hamlet,
     you may fade into the night—
But there is no doubt in vale or glen,
        Sir Algernon's on site!

Sir Algernon's a handsome hound,
  he's muscular and strong;
His look is keen and ardent and
  his gaze, intense and long.
His brow is furrowed deep in thought,
  his senses are well-honed;
His coat is shiny and ship-shape,
  his fur is neatly combed.
He bobs his head from side to side
  while sniffing down the lane;
And when you think he's lost the trail,
  he finds it once again.

Sir Algernon, Sir Algernon,
  there's no one like Sir Algernon
For he's a cop in canine form,
  who watches all the goings-on
You won't meet him in a backstreet,
  on a boat or on some flight—
But when there is wrongdoing then
              Sir Algernon's on site!

He's gracious and well-thought-of,
    he's always on his guard.
And he's memorized details of every
    plot and patch and yard.
And when a home is burgled, or a
    necklace has been nabbed,
Or a cache of bones is missing, or
    a poodle has been grabbed,
Or the shop window is broken, and
    the culprits are in flight—
You'll never have to worry for
        Sir Algernon's on site!

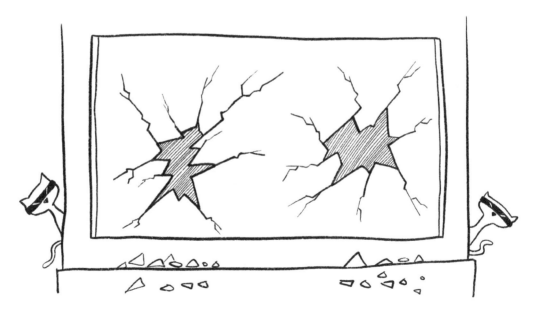

And when the peace is threatened for
      a truce has gone askew,
Or the President has lost some plans
      and chaos has ensued,
Be it missing secret folders, or
      code by the gigabyte—
If there's any need for scrutiny—
              Sir Algernon's on site!

And when the crime has been resolved,
      the Government will say:
"We're thankful for Sir Algernon,
      he always saves the day!"
You'll be sure he won't be resting
      on his laurels or his rear
For the very thought of lawlessness,
      can siphon all his cheer...

Sir Algernon, Sir Algernon,
    There's no one like Sir Algernon
His skill at catching criminals
    is worthy of a champion.
No matter if the alibi is
    foolproof or airtight;
If there's a whiff of wrongdoing—
        Sir Algernon's on site!

The world is full of scallywags who
    think they can't be foiled
There are rascals by the thousands who
    spread chaos and turmoil
But Sir Algernon will stop them all
    so let's give a *"Hurrah!"*
For Super Sleuth Sir Algernon:
    the Keeper of the Law!

Author's Note: If you enjoyed this poem, find and read the delightful poetry book *Old Possum's Book of Practical Cats* by T.S. Eliot.

TOTAL RECALL

I'm really no good at recalling
The things that I somehow cannot
So how come I always remember
That somehow there's things I forgot?

NEW ERA

I'm solving the world's water problem
And launching an era of hope
I'm cleaning the world's dirty water
By washing it deftly with soap!

PROPERLY PINK

I only eat porridge that's properly pink
    With splotches of purples and blues
When stirred with a spoon
It should quiver in tune
    And shimmer with delicate hues

I only eat porridge that's perfectly smooth
    And shiny and soft to the touch
When chopped with an axe
It should part like warm wax
    Resisting, but only so much

I only eat porridge that grows on a vine
    Whose pedigree is Japanese
When sniffed with a nose
It should smell like a rose
    With traces of limburger cheese

If only you'd bring me some porridge like that
I'd eat it with gusto and haste
And until you bring me some porridge like that
Expect me to dislike the taste!

BEAU PEEP'S SHEEP

Into the wee hours of the night
Ms. Beau Peep stewed and sweated
Her sheep were lost – out of her sight!
She agonized, she fretted!

Come morning, as a last resort
She went down to the station
And filed a missing-sheep report
With ample trepidation

The call went out in bounds and leaps
And soon, much to her comfort
A wolf was nabbed with all her sheep
(The sheep were safe and unhurt)

"A wolf led all your sheep away",
The constable reported
"No wolf could lead my sheep astray!"
A stumped Ms. Peep retorted

"He donned your dress, wore your perfume
And looked all sweet and frllly"
"He mimicked me?" Ms. Beau peep fumed
"Could my sheep be so silly?"

"Yes, sheep do cast a wary eye
And treat wolves with much loathing.
This time your sheep were hoodwinked by...

...A Wolf in Peep's clothing"

HOUSE OF CARDS

Build a house of cards, they said
It's not very hard, they said
Prop them up in twos and threes
But no one told me...

...**NEVER** SNEEZE!

ALWAYS ON DUTY

When a cake or pie goes missing
When they've lost another ball
When a vase is knocked and broken
When there's mud inside the hall
When the homework's torn or eaten
When a smudge adorns the wall
I'll be here to do my duty
I'll be here to take the fall
LoveMeFeedMeHugMePatMe
And I'll serve you well, that's all.

71

MASTER OF MONSTROSITIES

I'm the master of monstrosities
I make in my backyard
Using artificial hormones and
The stuff people discard

Such as medicines and cleaners
Such as hairspray, glue, and gunk
Mixed with plastic, toxic, manmade
Goops of chemical-ly junk

My potent vats of slushy slop Transmogrify with just one drop!

I've grown giant grinning spiders
Newts and worms that glow galore
Things with whiskers and appendages
That snore and soar and spore

Things that wriggle, wiggle, squiggle
Things that flutter, flail, and fly
Things that dribble, drool and drivel
Things that ooze and seep and sigh

But the weirdest thing of wonder
That my backyard ever grew...

...Is the creature I turned into
When I fell into my goo!

TRANSPORTATION

Catch a subway, catch a train
Catch a rocket, catch a blimp
Catch a bus or catch a plane
Catch a camel with a limp

Catch a ferry, catch a ship
Catch a trolley, tram, or van
Catch a taxi on a trip
Catch a wagon when you can

Catch them far or catch them near
Long or short or big or small...

...Once you catch them bring them here...

...We will gladly buy them all!

THE OVIRAPTOR'S KIN

Said Oviraptor to his kin,
  'I'm great at stealing eggs!
My arms are perfect—long and thin!
  I have the fastest legs!'

'My face has got a cunning look
  My gait is sly and keen
I steal those eggs by hook or crook
  My getaways are clean'

Ovi-Raptor: A species of Dinosaur originally named for it's (unjustified) reputation for stealing eggs from other dinosaurs

'And once an egg falls in my hands
  I cannot help but smile
The eggs from many Dino-lands
  I've added to my pile'

'No Oviraptor can compare
  Its stash of eggs to mine
A hoard this size has to be rare
  And none could be as fine'

But as he gloated, full of pride,
  He erred and turned his back
Which let his kin
              sneak by his side...

...And run off with his stack!

* Apparently the Oviraptor forgot his kin is also an Oviraptor!

A COLD TO END ALL COLDS

I'm hacking and coughing and sniffling
My sneezes are blowing down mountains and trees
I'm rattling and leaking and whiffling
The piles of used tissues are up to my knees

My eyes are all puffed up and bleary
My head feels as dense as my chest feels compressed
The back of my throat is all teary
The piles of used tissues are up to my chest

My nose is all gloppy and goopy
I've scrubbed it and rubbed it till it's raw and red
I'm feeling all   hazy and loopy
   The piles of   used tissues are
                                       over my
                                          he... lp!

A NIGHT LIKE THIS

The sun goes down, the word goes round
  And soon the packs of canines come
Oooh la la la, a big Gala,
  Where pooches gather with their chums

There's food and song for four-pawed throngs
  A shindig that no mutt will miss
This raucous loud wild-doggie crowd
  Has never seen a night like this...

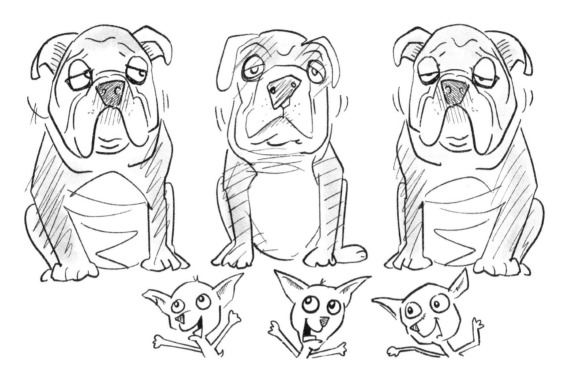

The Chihuahuas yip hip-hurrahs
    They're waiting for the band to play!
The Bulldogs pout and shake their snouts
    They're just not feeling quite as gay!

A pack of Pugs chug on their mugs
    They wag their tails, they reminisce
The howls and barks fill up the dark
    For no one's seen a night like this…

All hear the Hound's smooth silky sound—
  He serenades and croons the moon
Close by Great Danes will entertain
  By tooting on their big bassoons

The Pekinese all chomp for cheese
  They want some cheddar, and some swiss!
Big bones to chew, some old shoes too
  Yes no one's seen a night like this...

The Malamutes groove on their flutes
  The Collies chase their tails nearby
The Saint Bernard's play games of cards
  Their muzzles clenched—the stakes are high!

Prim Poodles waltz all through the vaults
  They're lost in dainty dancing bliss
As midnight chimes, it's happy times
  For no one's seen a night like this...

The Dalmatians still love to run
   And romp and gambol, frisk and play
The Beagles sniff for one last whiff
   Of what's left of the grand buffet

This night was fun but soon the Sun
   Will exit from its dark abyss
So *au revoir*, dear Moon and Star,
   We've never seen a night like this!

It's end of show, friends, take it slow
   Yes, no one's seen a night like this!

"It's time to go!"

        "Oh yes we know!"

So hard to leave a night like this!

MY OPPOSITE

One day I met my opposite
We stood and stared non-stopposite
We were so unlike each-other
I thought my head would popposite

So I proposed a swapposite
Let's switch our lives flip-flopposite
If you are me and I am you
We'll both come out on topposite

And now that I'm
my opposite
I so regret our swapposite
For everything I try to do
I end up doing the opposite

I wake up when I go to sleep
I giggle when I try to weep
I smile when I am feeling sad
I'm pleasant when I'm feeling mad
I sit down when I try to walk
I clam up when I try to talk
I goof off when I try to work...
When I am calm I go berserk!

So if you meet your opposite
And you're tempted to swapposite
The only thing I'll say to you
Is RUN!
And
DO NOT
STOPposite!

88

ON AND ON

I built a little robot
My robot built two more
And then each robot cloned itself
And soon I had a score

A score of eager robots
Scavenging all they find
And turning every bit and bolt
Into more of their kind

And soon a million robots
Went streaming out my door
And now the world is overrun
From mountaintop to shore

I've learnt my robot lesson
I've figured out my glitch
Henceforth the robots that I make
Must feature an 'off' switch.

MONSTERVERSE

Up the shore and
Down the coast
Vampires fear their
Dentist most

Werewolves shed a
Lot of hair
Clogging bathtubs
Everywhere

Witches brewing
Witches brew
Looks like "Ugh!" and
Tastes like "Ewww!"

Zombies shuffle
Down the street
Loving every
Brain they meet

Ogres only
Grunt and *Roar*
A chat with them
Is sure to bore

Poltergeists
Are somewhat shy
If you scare them
They will cry

LORD OF THE BUBBLES

Every bubble that you see
That ever was or yet shall be...

Bubbles in the
foamy sea?
Bubbles in your
bath or tea?

Bubbles floating
in the sky?
Bubbles that you
rent or buy?

Trapped in ice
or lava-hot?
Spawned from soup
or soap or snot?

Blown from
well-chewed bubble-gum?
Or just fizzing in
some scum?

All the bubbles that you chase
Here on earth or outer space
Rise and fall at my command
Dutiful to my demands

When I raise my hands and stop...?
Somewhere scads of bubbles pop!
When I shake my head or hair...?
Elsewhere bubbles fill the air!
When I tug my nose or ear...?
Bubbles burst and disappear!
When I tap my toe or knee... ?
All your bubbles rush to me!

From the caves and from the coves
Bubbles swarm to me in droves!
When I disco-dance or groove
Bubbles orbit my each move!

I'm the Bubble Lord you see
Bubbles all belong to ME!

**They're MINE! MINE! MINE!
All MINE!**

And someday...

Someday when the world is lax
I'll make you pay a BUBBLE TAX!

And you will owe me lots of dough
For every bubble that you blow
For every bubble that you see
That ever was and yet shall be ... !

And I'll be RICH, **SO RICH**!!!

BETTY THE YETI

Way up in the mountains where none dare to go
Sweet Betty the Yeti abides in the snow
She scales all the scarps and caresses the crags
She faces the freeze in a dress made of rags

She lives in a cavern and sleeps on a rock
She munches on moss while daydreaming of socks
She draws on the cave walls with old bits of bone
Her pets are a snowman, two sticks, and a stone

She rarely gets letters or parcels or mail
(It's quite hard to find her so veiled is her trail)
Her cousin, the Bigfoot, will sometimes come by
They'll play cards and checkers and snack on moss-pie

I met her one winter when I lost my way
She found me and fed me and saved me that day
So gentle her manner, so caring her heart
I gave her my socks in exchange for moss-tart

She's shy as a dormouse and keeps out of sight
She only forages on dark moonless nights
She's happy to be by herself in the snow
Way up in the mountains where none dare to go.

COURAGE

Sprain an ankle? Pop an elbow?
Scrape a shin or skin a knee?
Insect bites and little splinters?
None of these can fluster me!

Upset tummy? Bump on forehead?
Fever? Rashes? Ache in ear?
Things that take me to the doctor
Those are not the things I fear!

ULP!

TABLE MANNERS

Some use chopsticks,
 Some use forks
Some use spoons and
 Some use sporks
Some use fingers,
 Some their nose
Me? I like to
 use my toes!

MORNING STRIKE

We're having a strike, we're making a fuss
We're griping about our morning school bus
We think it's unfair; we find it a crime
Our school bus is always, always on time

How neat it would be, how nifty, how cool
If it was delayed, we'd miss us some school!
We'd get to sleep in, not stand here irate!
Oh why won't our school bus *ever* be late?!?

A DREAM

I dreamed a dream of sunny skies
Of popsicles and apple pies
Of chasing golden butterflies
A wonderland so full of joys,
        I dreamt it twice and thrice

While dreaming of this paradise
Perhaps I made some oohs and sighs
Some giggles, laughs, some jolly cries
(They say I made a LOT of noise)
        And now ...

... I pay the price!

DEEP THOUGHTS

Said the Gnu as it gnawed on a knot,
"I keep gnawing this knot but for what?
    I thought gnawing a knot
    Is conducive to thought
But my gnawed-knot gnu-thoughts
                    add to naught"

WISH YOU WERE HERE

I sit and watch
  a spider spin its web
I sit and watch
  the water flow and ebb
I sit and watch
  the growing of the grass
I sit and watch
  the seasons as they pass
If you were here
  I'd share all this with you
These joys of sitting
  stuck on super glue

A RIDDLE

Answer me this riddle please:
What has three eyes, tends to sneeze?
Two horns, black stripes, spiky tail
Bat-like wings and shell of snail?
Fangs of doom and stubby legs?
Fishy smell, lays rotten eggs?
Peppered with pink polka dots?
Oozes slimy trail and trots?
Floppy ears and hairs a mess?
Simple answer, can you guess?
It's the creature that's designed...

...By fourth-graders, all combined.

THE BARE BEAR
A Tongue Twisterrrrr

"I can barely bear this winter"
Brrrrr-d a bored bare bear
As he plucked burrs off his bear fur
In his bored-bear chair

"No one's going to come here bearing
Clothes for bears to wear
I must bear the bare-bear burden
Not to be so bare"

So he wove a robe of burrs which
He then wore with care
And the burred bored bear no longer
Was a bare Brrrrr-d bear

MEAN BEAN
*Song of the
Mischievous Imp*

I'm a mean bean
I'm a foul owl
I will sulk, skulk
As I prowl, scowl

I will *Eek! Squeak!*
I will slide, stride
I will romp, stomp
I will glide, hide

I will haunt, taunt
I will leap, creep
I will howl, growl
While you sleep deep

You might think, blink,
You can see me
But you don't, won't!
I'm a wee flea

I will stay, play
All my slick tricks
Make a mess, yes
Play a trick, quick

I will snag, drag
All your tid-bits
I will shake, make
Things go *Spritz! Fritz!*

You will fret, yet
I will toil, roil
I will hex, vex
I will soil, spoil

You will cry *Why?*
You'll be sad, mad
I won't care, there
I'm a bad cad!

I'm no wimp imp
I've a keen gene
I'm a champ scamp
I'm a mean bean

I'm a mean bean
I'm a mean bean
Just a teeny tiny little
Mean bean!

POTION FOR A MATH TEST
(or Why I Got An 'F' in Math)

"First, take one scritch of monkey's itch,
And swirl in swish of pirate's blade
Then add a dab of dragon scab,
And spice with hints of tint of jade

Whip up the scowl of two foul owls,
And pep with pinch of poet's woe
Mix in the roar of ogre's snore,
And boil this all with stub of toe!"

"And when you're done", the Wizard hummed,
"You will have made a potent brew—
A potion with the notion to
Resolve whatever's vexing you

No time to think! I cooked this drink!
And poured it on my test today!
Well, did my test turn out the best?!?
No …

….it grew wings and flew away! :(

THE GLOOMY CLOWN

The Super Duper Circus Troupe
  Is trooping into town
 They're singers and they're acrobats
 They're dancers and they're gym-a-nasts
And in the midst
  Of all the glitz
    We see a gloomy clown.
    His smile is upside down!

The Super Duper Circus Troupe
  Is setting up a show.
 For juggling and for trap-e-zing
 For singing, dancing, waltz-a-zing
Their earnest smiles
  Exude for miles
    Except that gloomy clown
    Whose smile is upside down!

The Super Duper Circus Troupe
  Is entertaining us.
  With music, dance and magic tricks
 And craziness that's gi-gan-tic
They're rollicking
  And frolicking
   And here's that gloomy clown!
   His smile? Still upside down!

   The Super Duper Circus Troupe
    Is heralding their star!
    Although his countenance is grim
    That only makes us laugh with him
   His jaunt, his wit
    Has us in splits
     We love the gloomy clown!
     Whose smile is upside down!

The Super Duper Circus Troupe
Is packing up their tents
They gave us such a super show
We're sorry that they have to go
And though we cheer
It's rather clear
We'll miss the gloomy clown!
Whose smile is upside down!

THE GENIE'S LAMENT

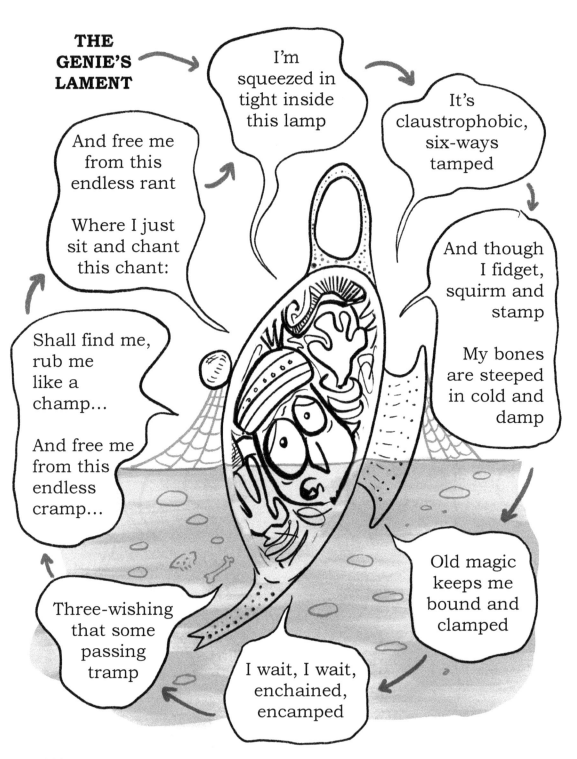

I'm squeezed in tight inside this lamp

It's claustrophobic, six-ways tamped

And though I fidget, squirm and stamp

My bones are steeped in cold and damp

Old magic keeps me bound and clamped

I wait, I wait, enchained, encamped

Three-wishing that some passing tramp

Shall find me, rub me like a champ...

And free me from this endless cramp...

And free me from this endless rant

Where I just sit and chant this chant:

WORM, MISS

Now... if you find a worm, Miss
Upon your epidermis
You needn't squeal or squirm, Miss
Or think of little germs, Miss
Just use a grip that's firm Miss
And pick that little worm, Miss
Then put it in your thermos
And I'll gladly confirm, Miss
That when Mum finds the worm, Miss
She'll give you better lunches
Till the end of your school term, Miss

SLURPIE

Said the Aardvark, as she put on her pants
"I feel famished from feeding on ants
    Each ant is so slight
    It is barely a bite
So I'm off to slurp up some eleph-ants"

NOWHERE

Nowhere is a place I know
Where no one ever goes
A somewhere-out-there kind of place
Which no one really knows

To get to it you first get lost
Then follow your own nose
And if you do that long enough
You'll find it I suppose

And if you tell a friend or two
You might find they're aghast
For no one really likes to hear
You're going nowhere fast

HACKER-WOCKY: A Parody Poem
With Apologies to Lewis Carroll

'Twas brillig, and the online memes
   Did gyre and gimble in the code:
All mimsy were the music streams,
   As web-comments upload.

"Beware the Internet, my child!
   The sites that snare, the blogs that catch!
Beware the viral vids, and shun
   The frumious download-patch!"

She took her vorpal mouse in hand;
   Long time the manxome Web she surfed
So rested she by an old selfie
   And stood and scanned the turf.

And, as in uffish thought she griped,
   The Internet, with eyes of flame,
Came whiffling through the broadband pipe
   And burbled at this game!

Author's Note: Make sure to find and read the wonderful nonsense poem *Jabberwocky* penned by Lewis Carroll in his book *Through the Looking Glass!*

One, two! One, two! And through and through
    The vorpal mouse went click and clack!
The Web went down, and with no frown
    She went galumphing back.

"And hast though slain the Internet?
    Come to my arms, my beamish child!
O frabjous day! Callooh! Callay!"
    He chortled as if wild.

'Twas brillig, and the online memes
    No longer gimbled in the code:
All mimsy were the silent streams,
    No web-comments upload.

Meanwhile...

THE INTERNET IS DOWN

We feel frantic, we feel manic
Our despair is past galvanic
It's a World Wide Web of panic
    For the Internet is down…

"Check Your Internet Connection!"
We encounter firm rejection
When attempting web-detection
    For the Internet is down…

Even though they've been rebooted
All our gadgets sit here muted
Disconnected, uncomputed
    For the Internet is down…

Staring in a hushed compunction
We are baffled at this junction
All our Apps refuse to function
    For the Internet is down…

No more snapping, chatting, gabbing!
No more free downloads for grabbing!
No more e-coupons for nabbing!
    For the Internet is down...

No more surfing! No more tweeting!
No emoticon-ic greeting! :(
Here we sit now, overeating,
    For the Internet is down...

No more LIKE-ing, no more SHARE-ing
No more ALL-CAPS RANTING, SWEARING
WHO KNEW SILENCE IS SO GLARING!
    For the Internet is down...

No more impassioned debating
Not one comment, not one rating
Spinning cursors ... Endless waiting ...
    For the Internet is down...

No more music streams are queuing!
No more cat videos for viewing!
What, oh what, should we be doing?
    For the Internet is down...

We need input or the plumbing
In our heads will keep on numbing...
Help! The dark ages are coming!
    For the Internet is down ...

Help us! Save us! We're imploring!
Don't ignore this grave outpouring
OMG – LIFE'S MUCH TOO BORING!!!!
    When the Internet is down...

We're so bored our brains are shorting!
All our neurons are contorting!
Help us! Save us! We're re...

    What? It's back?!?

    Ok, never mind.

MRS. McCREE

The scourge of the oceans,
 the dread of the sea
The bane of the pirates
 was Mrs. McCree

All over the new world
 in ports wild and free
They trembled on hearing
 the name of McCree...

When told she was coming
 they'd scatter and flee
They'd forsake their treasure
 and forswear their tea
They'd scuttle their vessels
 and cling to debris
They'd seek out the sirens!
 Walk planks! Mutiny!
To *Davy Jones Locker* they'd
 dive one, two, three
Anything, oh anything,
 but Mrs. McCree...

SAFE!

Now who was this lady
 who made them knock-kneed?!?

She wasn't a sailor
 or brave enlistee
No swashbuckling rascal
 who oozed villainy
No brigand, no bandit,
 no outlaw was she
No soldier of fortune
 was Mrs. McCree...

No, Mrs. McCree was...
 simply matronly
And made pirates be how
 they'd rather not be!

Like having to wash up
  and wear clean undies
And shampoo their dreadlocks
  and braid their goatees
And eat with utensils
  and do their laundry
And mind all their manners,
  their Q's and their P's
She'd scold them, she'd nag them,
  she'd spank their *heinies*
For that was her mission,
  her calling, her '*Qi*'
Whatever it took, yes,
  to clean up the sea...

The scourge of the ocean,
 the dread of the sea
Motherly, Matronly,
 Mrs. McCree.

STAY CLEAR

There's this place that's never sunny
 Somewhat stale, with touch of mold
Damp and dark, it smells like bunnies
 That are perplexingly old

It has slowly been bombarded
 With a deluge of refuse
Long forgotten, disregarded
 Where the crud of time accrues

Should you chance to find yourself here
 You might unwillingly gag
So I must insist you stay clear
        Of the bottom
          of my bag.

THE HATCHING OF ROBOTS

The hatching of robots is a delicate job
  It isn't just one of your everyday tasks
You need whatchamacallits and thingumabobs
  And doohickeys, doodads and duct tape and masks

You need patience, precision, perfection in poise
  A room that is tepid, just so and no more
You must whisper and tiptoe, make no sound or noise
  It's ok to nap, but be sure not to snore

You must wash your hands thrice, disinfect all your stuff
  You must dress like an astronaut, visor and all
You must filter the air of all traces of fluff
  And then nestle each robot egg in a soft shawl

Then you sit back and wait for the eggs to chime thrice
  They will click, hiss and whirr and start glowing in spots
Soon the shell shall shear sharply, as if neatly sliced
  And then out will emerge your new gaggle of bots.

135

I MET A MAN WITH TWENTY HEADS

I met a man with twenty heads
He said "A few are still in bed
I have so much upon my mind
That sometimes some get left behind

"But do not think I am a dunce
For I think twenty thoughts at once
And when my heads collaborate
The outcomes are elaborate

"We probably could solve *World Peace*
Bring *Climate Change* down to its knees
End *Poverty*, and *Hunger* too!
Oh, yes, there's so much we can do!

"We'll get to it one day you'll see
As soon as all my heads agree
To stop arguing endlessly
On what to watch next on TV!"

FACT-O-PHOBIA

When I was just a little kid
To school I feared to go
I worried I might learn so much
My brain would over-flow
  And extra facts that I would hear
  Would surely leak out of my ears!

But all my teachers tell me now
I needn't have such fears
They're pretty sure that nothing will
Be exiting my ears
  They're firmly certain, they explain,
  They've learnt I've got a fact-proof brain!

STILL CAN'T SLEEP

When you're tossing, when you're turning
And your tired brain is yearning
   For a morsel of a
          smidgen of some sleep
You can twist and twirl and tumble
You can grimace, gripe and grumble
   But the more you writhe the
          less the rest you reap

And as slumber and you scuffle
Locked in cha-cha, tango, shuffle
   You might persevere and
          make that wished-for leap
When at last descends the curtain
Only one thing is for certain
   That the moment that you doze off...

UNI-CORN

Said the Unicorn, as she eyed her long horn
"Oh my horn is as sharp as a thorn
    Which I don't mind at all
    Except late in the Fall
When I'm dashing through fields full of corn..."

ERNIE DINKO

Ernie Dinko was a stinko
Never took a bath or two
So much dirt had settled on him
He was inches deep in goo

This attracted flora, fauna
Sprouting seeds and bushes too
Ecosystems fell in place and
Soon he was a walking zoo

Rabbits nested in his pockets
Squirrels frolicked, pheasants flew
Predators preyed in his tresses
Lurking where the grasses grew

There were claims of panda sightings
There were claims of herds of gnu
There were rumors of Koalas
Wallabies and Kangaroo

"Habitats are under danger!"
Ernie would say in *Urdu*
"I am helping Mother Nature!
Won't you try to help her too?"

So convincing was his message
We all followed in his shoes
Now we are a world of stinkos
We don't mind so why do you?

MUMS VS. MICE

Now Mice are known to squeak and dash
And scurry, scamper in a flash
As endlessly they search for trash
  And tidbits they can nibble

Their eyes are big, their ears are wide
They hug the walls when they're inside
The smallest clatter makes them hide
  Without the slightest quibble

Now Mums we know are warm and bold
They're grown-up tall with hearts of gold
And even if they nag or scold
  Who's fiercer than a mother?

Since Mums are bigger than most mice
You'd think it would be no surprise
To guess who gets most traumatized
  When they chance on each other!

THE BORROWER

You should be glad that I brought back your shoe
(Hope you don't mind there's a new hole or two...)

You should be glad that I brought back your shirt
(Hope you don't mind there's a few flecks of dirt...)

You should be glad that I brought back your tie
(Hope you don't mind that it fell in a pie...)

You should be glad that I brought back your coat
(Hope you don't mind it was munched by a goat...)

But lend me no more – for I think you'll agree
Your stuff's become much too much shabby for me!

HOMEWORK EXCUSE

Late at night and up doing homework
Eyes all groggy, face all scowled
All that thinking made me hungry—
How my stomach grumbled, growled!

Everyone was sleeping soundly
I would have to feed myself!
Though I searched I could not find a
Bite of food on any shelf

I was feeling fully famished
I felt dizzy, hazy, weak
Not one crumb or scrap or tidbit?
Could my prospects be more bleak?

I don't know what happened next as
I was in a fuzzy fog
Did my dog chew up my homework?
Uhm, you see, we have no dog...

THE MOUNTAINEER

The mountaineer adjusts his gear,
  Stares at the peaks and sighs
"For twenty years I've base-camped here
  Where massifs kiss the skies

   "My joints have turned a trifle stiff
    Counting the days and nights
   Until I scale this craggy cliff
    And savor its delights

"Past crevice, crevasse, cleft I'll hop
  To plant my flag on high
Take selfies on that snowy top
  Against a cobalt sky

  "For twenty years, with ready pack,
    This dream dazzles my sights
    The only thing that holds me back?
    My pesky fear of heights...!"

ODE TO THE
BEST DARN POEM
WOT I EVER COMPOSED

I marveled when you first emerged,
A tendril of a thought
You needed care and nurturing:
I gave you all you sought

I watched you thrive and blossom and
Unfurl your worded wings
The texture of a language,
Vibrating in your strings

I felt your rhythms synchronize,
Your meters coalesce
I sensed your feet a-dancing as
You took on loveliness

Your metaphors? Magnificent!
Your similes? A bliss!
The way your words caressed my tongue
Was no less than a kiss!

A masterpiece so perfect that
No world could be the same!
I went to bed so sure I stood
Upon the cusp of fame

I dreamt all night how you and I
Would be changing mankind
I woke up—to be horror-struck—
You'd faded from my mind! :(

Oh why, oh why, did I commit
The poets greatest sin?
I should have put you to paper,
While you were still within!

I've tried, but failed, to bring you back—
I'll mourn you ever more
You could have been my *'Raven'* but
Instead you're...

NEVERMORE!

Author's Note: *The Raven* is a famous poem by Edgar Allan Poe.

TOOTERS

Do you... want to hear music that isn't too grand?
That does not make use of the foot or the hand?
That sounds somewhat nasal and just a tad bland?
Then come hear our hooting nose-tooting rock band!

Do you... dislike the sound of guitars when they're strummed?
And loathe hearing pianos and violins and drums?
But sounds of kazoos have you clapping your hands?
Then come hear our hooting nose-tooting rock band!

Do you... like burping tubas and raspy bassoons?
Are patient when melodies drift out of tune?
Then come see what wonders our noses command!
Then come hear our hooting nose-tooting rock band!

RESTLESS BREEZE

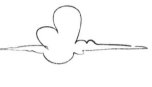

She rushes in
Then softly ebbs
She plucks a tune
On spider webs

She hovers with
The dragonfly
And chases clouds
Across the sky

With tender hands
And nimble feet
She dances with
Each mote she meets

She surges through
The cracks and nooks
And plays a game of
Tag with brooks

O Restless Breeze
Come to me too
For I have brought
A gift for you

My gift is yours
To take for play...

...I hope you'll blow it
Far away!

THE ANXIOUS PARENTS

Well... your... Math is fairly feeble
And your Language Arts are weak
And your Science needs improving
Twice as much as Ancient Greek!

And your Handwriting is sloppy,
While your Diction makes us flinch...
And every time we lecture you,
You doze off in a pinch!

You don't *ever* do your homework –
And you barely seem to care
All your lax and lazy habits
Simply fill us with despair

Here we're prepping you for college –
But you'd rather sip your juice??? ....

...Yes, we know you're just a Baby,
   But – gee! – that's a lame excuse!!!

THE GHOST OF
HUMPTY DUMPTY

The ghost of Humpty-Dumpty
Still perches on *that* Wall
And ponders, frumpty-grumpty
That infamous BIG FALL

And wonders why those King's men,
With bumbling equine crew,
Who rushed to put him back again
Brought not one drop of glue.

SIDEKICK

Ahoy there friendly *Alien*!
Please come down from the stars
And take me on your spaceship if
You're headed off to Mars

I long to see the Galaxy
From shore to starry shore
I daydream I can leave this place
Where everything's a chore

I wish to soar through Outer Space
To Saturn's rings and moons
The thought I'll high-five Pluto always
Makes me want to swoon

I'll work hard for my passage and
I'll wield a mop and broom
(I'd rather sweep a spaceship than
Be forced to clean my room!)

There's homework that needs doing but
I'm finding it's a bore
The Universe keeps asking me
To come out and explore

So hey there friendly Alien
Please come down from afar...

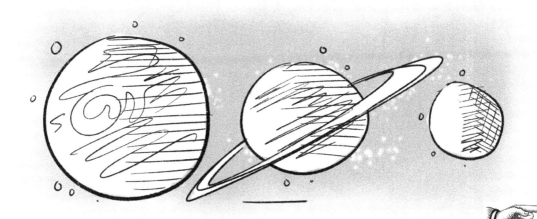

...And let me be your sidekick as you
    Travel star to star

HANDY CANDY

Mister Andy made some candy
But his candy was not dandy
So he canned his awful candy
And he sent it to Miss Mandy
Said Miss Mandy "This is grand-y
But I think the texture's bland-y
Let me make your candy sandy
Shape it nicely, bowed and bandy
Then it won't be just some candy
But a tool that's also handy!"

And that is how
You too can now
Come here and buy
Lick, use, or try:

ANDY - MANDY'S
HANDY - DANDY
SANDY - BANDY
GRANDY - CANDY

In Which Witches Gather
For Their Annual Family Picnic

Tonight's the night I ride my broom
And with brio I bravely zoom
   Through brooding sky and bramble
                To where gambol
               All my kin

Our brutish brouhaha is brash
We brusquely brawl and briskly clash
   (It's how we show affection
                And connection
               To our kin)

We gift each other gnats and rats
And wrinkly warts and bristly bats
   We make sure that each present
              Is unpleasant
                    For our kin

For fun we ZAP! and HEX! and JINX!
(We turn our Aunt into a Sphinx!)
   We're brazen, breezy, bratty–
              And so chatty
                   With our kin

We trade old potions, swap new spells
The air is bright with brackish smells
   We're yearning, burning, churning
          Magic-learning
            With our kin

Our brooding uncles hitch their pants
And burst into in a breathless dance
   And soon we're all contorting
          And cavorting
           With our kin

We brunch on bran and brie and brew
At break of dawn, we bid adieu
   Until next year we'll brandish
          Love outlandish
          For our kin!

SPELLING BEE

Our school an-nounced a 'Spell-ing Bee'
We all signed up so ea-ger-ly!
With thor-ough meth-od-ol-o-gy
We stud-ied et-y-mol-o-gy
We mem-o-rized word lists and more
We would be champs – we were so sure!

Then came a *BEE* who cast a *SPELL*
And turned us into bees as well!
Our shock soon changed into delight —
Goodbye dear school! And hello flight!

Now we all do as that Bee does
We flutter, flitter, fly and buzz
We glide and dart, we zip and zap
We swarm and soar and sip on sap

This fancy life is free of fuss
What's that? You want to be like us?
Well, sign up for a Spelling Bee —
And then? You'll have to wait and see...!

HUMDRUM

This poem is monotonous
And humdrum to the ear
Alliteration's absent and
No assonance to hear
     No change in rhythm, style or pace...
     No interplay of word or space...
Its irony will probably
  be just as bare next year

This poem's pretty colorless –
It lacks all style and flair
It's like a hippopotamus
That only stands and stares
     No metaphor, no simile...
     Why doth it sulk so dismally...?
This scarcity of imagery
  will trigger much despair

And whoever wrote this poem needs
  to have this verse repaired.

CLOSING NOTES

The squeaks have been pipped
The tips have been topped
The shapes have been shipped
The flips have been flopped

    The book has been stored
    The pan has been caked
    The sea has been shored
    The earth has been quaked

The tooth has been picked
The wise have been clocked
The side has been kicked
The bed has been rocked

    The plips have been plopped
    The duck has been billed
    The sticks have been chopped
    The foot has been hilled

The sight has been eyed
The light has been skyed
The time has now come
For good to be byed!

ABOUT THE AUTHOR

As a kid growing up in India, poet-artist Vikram Madan
failed miserably at having imaginary friends
and, instead, had to make do with playing with words and
drawings, a passion that ultimately led to his debut
award-winning book of funny poems, *The Bubble Collector*,
which is often compared to the works of Shel Silverstein.
An engineer by training, and a former award-winning
editorial cartoonist, Vikram currently lives near Seattle,
where he is now a professional artist and poet, and aspires,
through his whimsical paintings and funny poems,
to make the world a better place one
shared moment of levity at a time.

See more of Vikram's work at:

www.VikramMadan.com

Follow Vikram's Work Online
Look for **@ArtByVikram**

INDEX of TITLES

If you enjoyed this book, you will definitely enjoy:

'The Bubble Collector'

Funny Poems for All Ages 6 to 106

"Freewheeling... Punchy... Wisecracking... Impish... Screwball...

High-Spirited Read-Aloud" - *Publisher's Weekly*

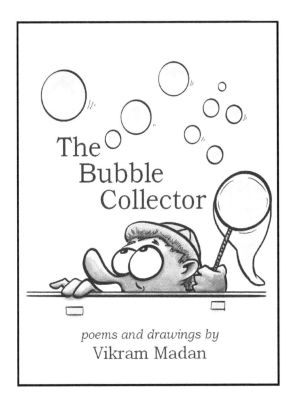

"Wonderfully illustrated... reminiscent of Dr. Seuss and Shel Silverstein... a great book for introducing children to the joys of poetry!"

"Funny... Sophisticated... As good as anything by Shel Silverstein!"

"Very reminiscent of Silverstein. Quirky and delightful rhymes matched by quirky and delightful illustrations!"

"Charming, Funny, Delightful!"

- ***SEATTLE AREA BOOKSELLERS***

"...Lively and Kid-Friendly..." - ***J. PATRICK LEWIS*** U.S. Children's Poet Laureate (2011-2013)

"...Will have you bubbling over with laughs... Sure to tickle your funny bone!" - ***DOUGLAS FLORIAN*** Acclaimed Poetry Author

"...A witty look at the world... Get a copy. Sit back and enjoy!" - ***DAVID L. HARRISON*** Award-winning Bestselling Author

- Winner of a **Moonbeam Award for Poetry**

- Nominated by invitation for the **2014 WA State Book Award**

- **5-Star Reader Reviews**

*148 Pages * Paperback*

Available Online and Through Booksellers

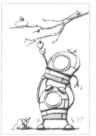

'A Rupture of Robots'

A Book of Robot Art by Vikram Madan

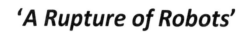

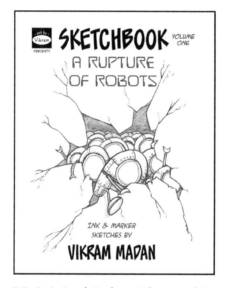

Over 80 Original Robot-Themed Drawings

178 Pages * Paperback

Available Online

Great gift item for anyone who likes

humor, art, robots, and coloring!

CPSIA information can be obtained
at www.ICGtesting.com
Printed in the USA
FSHW020619131221
86874FS

9 781986 885355